Gregory Warren Wilson
1996

Gregory Warren Wilson

PRESERVING
LEMONS

Staple
NEW WRITING
1996

PRESERVING LEMONS

Gregory Warren Wilson

ISBN 0 9510523 8 1

TYPESET
by
ROGER BOOTH ASSOCIATES
HASSOCKS, WEST SUSSEX
IN NEW BASKERVILLE

PRINTED
at
THE ARC & THROSTLE PRESS
NANHOLME MILL, TODMORDEN

DESIGN
by
BILL AND LUCY BERRETT

PUBLISHED
by
Staple NEW WRITING
15 JULY 1996

Staple
is published with
financial assistance
from East Midlands
Arts

For my parents

CONTENTS

LOVE POEM IN THE FORM OF A BRIGHT BLUE SOUP TUREEN

This is for you, from Poland, my love,
or rather from me.
It is not a subtle duck-egg blue,
not Dresden or Imperial,
but electric, sprigged improbably
with artichokes, harebells, foxgloves
picked out in gilt. Here
the ladle's mousehole is chipped,
and the lid is crowned with a curlicue
I had to re-glue.

But it is blue, blue as mad enamel,
a huge scoop of spangled heaven
from the firmament in a Byzantine tomb,
and it holds enough for twenty-two.
Open it – inside it's pale and smooth,
a freshwater oyster's mother-of-pearl,
glazed like my eyes, fired like my heart –
a vacuum which waited and waited all summer
for clarified consommé, compote of fruit,
all winter for leek and potato soup.

COLD KILN

Afterwards, she learnt to restore porcelain,
beginning with mug handles, teapot spouts;
but people heard and brought chipped jasper-ware,
faience, a Georgian chocolate pot.

She refused to take on much, declined
money, knowing that patience was her way
of overcoming the sheer
haphazardness of chance.

Her windowsills were lined with jagged shapes,
fragments of eggshell; things that could wait.
Bone china, being translucent, cast
soft shadows on her hands as they pieced
together the present, filed excrescences of glue,
regilded lustres rubbed to nothing.

She taught herself to dissemble
Spode – plates long-since broken
and clamped on the back with metal pins –
working with a surgeon's precision
on slipped discs.
The local museum wrote, complimenting
'her painstaking, exquisite touch –
a dangerous skill, verging on forgery.'

But the vessels she salvaged
always knew their volumes, once,
had spilt beyond definition;
greenstick fractures flawed
the inner profile of a shoulder,
or thickened in the throat.

And she knew, as she turned
famille rose in her hands,
how crazing spreads across enamel,
how blown glass, imperfectly annealed,
can shear a ring around its lip
with a noise like ice splitting in sunlight,
and would see her daughter's hand
under the glazed surface of the pond,
fissures like veins spreading away,
the pale underglaze blue;
would see herself, always at the rim,
her lips shearing off in the cold.

ENGLISH MINIATURIST

I do not execute likenesses
on thin tablets of ivory
the size of grand piano keys.

I do not take commissions, either,
for so-and-so's King Charles spaniel,
or retiring headmasters.

With my grey hair and erudition
I lecture at the V&A, on occasions;
I might look mousy but I am an authority

in my chosen field, and I chose it.
In my walled garden I grow old roses,
no new-fangled scentless Hybrid Teas.

By lamplight my hands are nearly translucent,
pale as the membranes of batwings,
cool as a nurse soothing a fever.

With these hands I wash my cashmere cardigan.
I never wear the single strand
of angel's-cheek coral I was given in Milan.

I have learnt to answer personal questions
like a mountain stream when quizzed
about its source – with a clear trickling laugh.

By the bath a glass jar preserves
gelatinous capsules in pastel shades;
scent seeps from them as they dissolve.

On sheets of cream paper, wove not laid,
I write with scarcely a correction,
with the dexterity of a wren

threading moss into a perfectly lined nest.
In this context, when I detect pretension,
I smash it, as cuckoos do eggs.

In some respects I am unshockable,
admiring Edo erotic woodblock prints;
on some mornings the librarian's ill-judged

blouse can knock the breath out of me,
leave me reeling. Aniline dyes.
With scarcely a correction I describe

the points at which conjecture intersects
with insight, insight with lies.
On my mantelpiece I keep

three Egyptian glass beads
from a necklace,
circa 2,500 BC, I believe.

DICTATING A LOVE LETTER

Write to him this;
write ...
              that the pomegranate tree
has turned grey with paper wishes
I have tied into its branches.

Write that whenever I see yellow
I think of him twitching the strings of his kite
as if he were the puppeteer of sunrise
and I the kite –
fidgety as the wind,
singing without a voice.

Write that my Peking robin is mute,
as if loneliness had snipped its throat
with a pair of nail scissors;
it will not drink even from celadon.

Write that I have been promised
the hair ornament with kingfisher feathers
and coral and two tiny silver fish.

Write it in brush-strokes
long and supple as grass-stalks in a spring wind;
write it as if you'd dipped your brush
in a moonlit lake.

Write it so the S-sounds
trail like silk over polished wood,
and show me
              show me where it says
how I catch my breath,
thinking of things to say,
how my eyelids are like fins
fanning away tears between the words.

Show me where. There? And there?

WE WERE SO BROKE

our gifts to each other were free –
a handful of bluebells stolen in the rain;
as I pulled, pale stems creaked, snapped
and oozed clear beads of sap. You,
in return, ran all the way from the tube
to my doorbell, and panted
through our first embrace of the day.

Later you gave me rare editions,
page-ends gilded against the dust, and I
brought back Chinese celadon for you,
goldfish swirling under jade glaze.

Then we grew to depend on trust
without tokens, having learnt so much
about exchange, about how best to touch
one another ... but now,

now that we need not seize each other's hand
greedily under conspiratorial tablecloths,
and can leave half a bottle of wine undrunk
without a twinge,
what I miss, but do not mention, is
a glassful of bluebells by the bed,
that breathless impact thumping my chest.

MESSAGES

No bonfire in my suburban garden, stoked
and damped to send a plume of signals
to your Georgian mews. Between us
(only twenty minutes on the tube)
are our schedules. So

you leave me messages on the machine –
Billie Holiday, Schubert Lieder, crossword clues.
Sometimes when I'm abroad you phone
simply to hear my outgoing voice, you say.
Unfailingly polite, the electronic valet
receives you at any hour, translates
your call into a tell-tale blink
red as a pupil caught in a flash.
Wink wink wink.

Without you, time recoils;
a blank spool.
            Rewinding
I find a few spliced messages –
remnants on a cutting room floor;
the point being what isn't there.

You, who choose your words
carefully as clothes, give yourself away
only in hesitations – silence frayed
with self-consciousness.

Is it worth waking you now to say
'Sleep well'? By morning
words will be stranded
in a rockpool of reticence,
the tide withdrawn and the shore at play,
wave after inconsequential wave.

Stupid with figures, I recall
memorising your number,
learning you by heart,
and the first time I trusted myself
enough to risk a finger
touching digits.

ANY OTHER WAY

He would not like it much, were I to say
it was his wrists, remembering his wrists
which tightened tiny draw-strings round my heart.

The photo in my fiddle-case of him in snow –
smiling huddled in a shabby coat – shows
why I love him. He would not have it so.

Who can resist the make believe
that keeps us at our best, glimpsed
by candlelight in antique mirrors,

or tousled by the sea, grinning ruggedly?
But it is not so. Today it snowed,
and I remembered him – his wrists

thin as plant stems, and his hands
opening in unprompted acts of kindness.
If I did not tell him, would he ever know

I thought of him today as it began to snow,
as whiteness made particular
each leaf I'd overlooked, as quietness

settled unobtrusively? Would he know
the snow made each frail cyclamen ache,
and that I would not have it any other way?

7 December 1995

THE WATER TABLE

Think of it, under London –
gelatin legs that will not set,
shingle embedded like chunks of pineapple;
a cloth of watered silk spread on the surface,
and places laid in slate and clay.

The terrace colludes in a mirage;
houses are not solid,
just an assemblage of empty cubes,
balanced and waterproof, rooms
lit every evening like an aquarium.

Ice in the freezer distils white noise
round tubes of coolant,
assuming a guise of hardness.

I adjust my city tread
as a sailor does on deck, anticipating
the lurch of an imminent wave,
the tilt of tides
sucking up to a porous moon.

Rain resents the jaggedness
that comes between falling and merging;
longs to settle into sea where cloud and wave
meet and are breathed through gills,
unimpeded bodies passing each into each.

Trowelling holes for tulip bulbs,
I expect the soil to weep like a wound,
to ooze when I tread, or bulge
somewhere else, like a water bed.

Peripheral vision, quick as cornflour,
thickens the quicksand borders.
Ferns uncurl in the Gulf Stream
like fronds of seaweed in the wind.
Behind my back, lawns liquefy.

THIN MEN

Their thinness is sudden.
They have appeared in London
suddenly – on escalators,
in Soho cafes, arm in arm.
It's not that they've become noticeable
like a new word which obtrudes
its newfound familiarity; they
are discreet, their razored hair
is neat, lies close to the skull,
their skin even closer.

They speak several languages at once,
fluently; one with their eyes,
another in jokes they exchange like tokens,
a third in medicinal Latin –
vocabularies polished like talismen.
Even their limbs are telling
sinuous commentaries.
Purposeful as wolves, scavenging time,
their lips lie close to the skull,
their tongues even closer.

The definition
of their muscles is wasting,
wasted – articulated
by stamina and fatigue. Above
the last vertebra of their necks,
a hollow that would fit a gull's egg,
and at their temples
two shallow spoons scoop away.
Words live close to the skull,
their breath even closer.

SELF-MADE MEN

Just look: men in designer vests –
cotton Lycra snug as snug round silicone pecs –
are cruising Old Compton Street, W1.

Scooping chocolate-speckled spume
from unsweetened cappuccinos, they
choreograph each spoon's ellipse
and notice everything, but their lips
are guarded as a basalt Pharaoh.
They give nothing away
until they give themselves,
pair off and re-group.

These men have remodelled themselves
in the image of man: you can see
they work out several times a week –
punishing, rewarding, routines. Some
have endured the after-sting
of a frozen nipple's piercing.
Initiation, like grooming, begins
with a razor nick – shaving a scrotum.

Arm in arm and territorial, they flaunt
tribal Ray Bans and stainless steel studs
instead of nose-pieces, quills, boars' tusks.

Would a Tattoo Parlour's syringe
and the chafe of latex clothing
irritate an Aborigine who'd bartered pain
for a cicatrix, standing proud –
who'd rubbed ash into a flyblown wound?

Straddled on high stools these Soho men
eye up the night's disingenuous prey;
courtship is urgent – a ritual
which ends in a take-away. They think
being young and irresistible is divine,
and do not care if their insouciant parade
tempts the savagery of middle age.

They know the ropes and the bouncers
at Club Adonis, Café Apollo;
why look further? – here's heaven. Overhead
the Milky Way, spilt sherbet,
fizzes through a sodium orange glare.
Underfoot, Leicester Square's sour turf
is shredded denim, threadbare.

GATEWAY TO INDIA
Bombay

Beauty Queens at the Taj Hotel order
mango milkshakes, chocolate milkshakes,
sip and gossip in fruit-salad English.

Their saris are bright as tablets of pigment
in a brand new enamel paintbox –
emerald, indigo, saffron, cochineal;
my tongue shapes and savours colour-words
silently on my palate as if they were
mint, lemon, cinnamon, vanilla.

'Miss Catwalk 94' is Gandhara sculpture,
familiar to me from fragments
in the British Museum,
and her gestures are sable
brushstrokes on ivory air.

Outside, the sun is low, a back burner
reducing light; night begins to caramelise.
Peanut sellers twist the evening's supply
of paper cones, and kindle wood in saucepans.
Blue smoke sharp as boning knives
slits and stings the nostrils passing by.

Pavements heaped with daylight trash –
earrings, bangles, silver anklets –
begin to glitter like fool's gold
by paraffin lamp; night-vendors light up
at dusk, punctual as fireflies.
They know their moment, and their values,
can gauge a pocket by the shoes,
and have learnt unspoken ways
of getting foreigners to choose.

THE MISSIONARY'S EEL

She kept it in a red plastic bucket
with just enough water to cover it.
The children came to look.
She treated their ringworm
and taught them modesty,
starting with shoes, then t-shirts;
a strategy ending with underwear.

She learnt enough of their language
to explain, firstly, what sea was,
then that deep in the sea there lived
conger eels which could bite
off fingers that played.
Born with a cleft palate,
she came to understand it
as a sign for her to overcome
the duplicity of language –
the snake's forked tongue.

The eel spiralled in its bucket,
secreting mucus;
the children dared each other to touch,
then squealed.

They knew how to kill a snake
by grasping it behind the jaw,
pinching its head closed with thumb and finger,
putting the whole head in their mouth
and pulling sharply; a clicky
dislocation.

But the missionary's eel was different;
she kept it.
She kept it in the shade.
At night it slithered into her dreams.

TECHNICIAN

I have never known such greed
for detail;
greed so famished it ingests
itself, its own tail.
                   Watch it

swerve and dissolve in the scrub,
brown along a branch, green in grass,
a string of zigzag diamonds
melting along its spine.
Watch it, now, lapping the libation
I pour into saucers.

Whatever draws its eye
it excretes – tepid skeletons,
mouse, fledgling, crushed eggshell.
But it flows on and on
hungering for warmth to clasp
inside its dislocating jaw,
to pass along its gut.

I must not slice it with the spade
but live with it,
give it house space;
let it hunt for me,
deliver its dead trophies, and admit

that as it feeds itself,
it tempts me
with a surreptitious skill.
Whatever fascinates it
it kills.

I write it up
in notebooks ruled in green ink;
line by line –
habits, behaviour, reflexes.

Binding my wrists in paper
skins it sheds,
I milk its syringe-teeth.

This is how serum is made
from venom – like poetry,
distilling intensity
clear drop by clear drop.

PRESERVING LEMONS

Their house smelt of hot lampshades,
chopped coriander, couscous.
Whatever the weather, Harry's grandmother
wore black; she'd come over from Cyprus
and was always in the kitchen,
or nowhere to be seen,
tending the inexplicable sores on her ankles.
When she spoke I didn't understand.
It didn't matter; Harry always answered back.

He got shingles in the summer term.
I used to visit after school,
grin at her in silence, and go on up.
But once she called out from the kitchen
as though I could understand. And I did,
at least while she was scrubbing lemons,
up to her wrists in a bobbing sinkful.

I watched her scour wax off rinds, cut deep
across each dimple where the stalk had been
(like for brussels sprouts) and stuff in salt.
Then she crammed them into sterile jars
hot from the oven, and poured on boiling water.

All the while, she talked to me, so
I told her what I'd told no-one –
my formula for invisible ink;
even told her that at night I wrote, dipping
a special pen in a test-tube of lemon-juice,
salting things away in pristine notebooks.

We both knew the other understood
more than the lemons, or the languages we spoke;
we shared a need to exchange recipes,
knew the importance of sharp kitchen knives, nibs,
tasted the zest, the sting of words,
and knew how to savour what others preserved.

A SPRIG OF CHILLIS

I send you poems like pale cheeses;
carefully moulded,
a whiff of sheepishness about them –
experience curdled and preserved
in tidy rinds, endstopped lines.

They travel well,
these demure English cheeses;
never cause a stink
of putrefaction, or blocked sinks.

The sprig of chillis you sent me
smoulders.
Seedpods pointy as stiletto heels
and patent-leather shiny
turn the kitchen into a red light district.
Shall I make *spaghetti alla putanesca?**

You lay out your needs on Tuscan sheets –
perishable soft-fruit on table linen.
Thumbing your letter, I thumb you
as if selecting the sweetest nectarine,
the juiciest melon, feeling for bruises –
deliberate, intent.

We've agreed on terms;
bartering packets of Earl Grey tea
and carefully turned phrases
for your temperament,
your unpredictable phases,
your glass jars of jam and jelly
distilled from fruits in an orchard where,
towards sunset on summer evenings,
famished mosquitoes whinge,
and at night a porcupine claws the gate's hinge.

* *Putana*: Italian slang for prostitute.
  Spaghetti alla putanesca: a hot Neapolitan dish.

ALERTED BY TOO EMPTY A MIRROR

This is me
in Venice among resonant furniture –
bedside cabinet, chest of drawers,
Rococo headboard – all handpainted
green as pistachio ice cream
and garnished with crystallised flowers.

As I unpack
my shirts set off a chain reaction
in the wardrobe's acoustic chamber;
metal coat-hangers ting as they swing,
triangles playing with themselves.

Once, in Quenca at an impressionable age,
I overheard *Under the Gideon's Bible
you'll find a list of local brothels.*
I always look, but never have.
(Nor do I forget.) Now
the drawer's chaste cleanliness
rebukes my curiosity.

Tomorrow I shall make small arrangements
with clementines, glass fish, the brass key –
a still life of picnic things and *objets trouvés* –
but at the moment emptiness is pressing,
tiresome as laboured connotations.

I move discreetly, a novice
in a Trappist Monastery,
sensitised to new sandals
and all that they betray.

TRAPPING A NERVE
For A J

This evening – humid enough to bring out the flying ants –
I thought of you, cutting a lime in two; or rather
the cutting and the thought were one
with the smell of rind and fresh lime juice.

In such a moment time twists back
on itself – a Möbius Strip: suddenly
I was in your flat, winter in Goldhawk Road,
standing gauche in front of the mahogany wardrobe
with bevelled mirrors and an amber glass handle,
having undressed by gas-fire light
with a teenage self-consciousness
(indestructible purple underwear) while you
brought a glass of water to the wicker bedside table
and in it floated a slice of lime.

I loved you selfishly: how else could I learn
that love and selfishness both pass
and return?
I skimmed you with kisses – you whose skin
was fragile as the skin on warm milk. But then,
what more was there? I'd wake and dress ...
and you knew better than to exact
promises you knew I'd break, then recollect.
And yet this sensation remains
faster and truer than words,
specific as a nerve.

If I could, would I choose to know
whether this instant, standing by the flywire
watching an electrical storm, a stage-set storm
with the silhouettes of palm leaves stiff as scissored cardboard
stabbing the stars, and the smell of fresh lime,
whether this, now, carries sufficient charge
to recur in twenty years, precipitated
by a flare in the light and the sour thrill of cut rind
from a tree which has not yet been sown?

ALIVE AND KICKING

Rehearsing new casts,
new blood, you get edged
out of the front row,
then along the second. 'We
just want to try out ... '
You learn their ways of putting things;
their repertoire of euphemisms.

Then some new-hatched chickolina
gets plucked out,
gets wafted about in the glare
like a peacock fan. Audiences love it;
who wants fairy tales debunked, anyway?
It's the business – the feigned arts –
and they pick it all up, quick as magpies,
learn what sort of flutter the critics like,
how to cope with the hype.

But I've heard them memorising verses,
thunking out the chorus key by key
on a practice-room piano,
and I can read their semaphore smiles –
makes you ache; expressions learnt
walking away from a duff audition
with a kipper-fingered accompanist,
the sort who'll set a tempo
to wrong-foot you. And leer.

Me? Got back into shape
after Jessica was born,
did class every day;
friend in wardrobe (on the quiet)
let out a seam here and there,
temporarily.

I watch the lambs, dark-eyed as astrakhan,
being led on, going one by one
to the producer's office to discuss
'understudies, contracts' – stunned.

But nearer the back, bit muttony now,
the ones who got looked over once
are getting overlooked. Remember them
cradling cappuccinos backstage,
gossiping all hours, living off take-aways,
whispering *cellulite* and shrieking on the stairs?
These days they get back quickly
to one bedroom flats in Earls Court,
and know a thing or two about sacrifice.

TERME DI SATURNIA
Siena

Our clothes watched us from the boulders as we bathed,
flattened ghosts envious of weightless motion.
Submerged to the neck, limbs loomed like huge fish
breasting the oily film which moonlight silvered –
a mirror-maker floating mercury on hot, dark glass.

By morning your necklace was sulphur-stained,
flashed metallic blue like antique spoons,
and the limpet hollow between your collar bones –
half a locket open to my tongue –
tasted of rockpools and silver foil.

TIME BEING

Who is more patronising than the young?
No-one. We are the ones who save them
from seeing themselves; from seeing
the dark at the end of the tunnel.

We smile at grudges they put aside,
at concessions they make for frailties
that have nothing to do with our selves.
Why do we turn into game old birds?

For them. But by the time they've learnt
how it feels, we will not be here to say
'These are things we never told you. So.
Now you know why, you won't either.'

Meantime we indulge them, strategise
with Valium, cheat at patience – we
who must face unflattering humilities
and the consolation of having a cataract

removed. They imagine we look forward
to their cheery bits of news and sexless kisses.
'Not wanting to tire us' they leave on schedule
but we were tired before they came,

tired of putting on the same brave face,
tired of the lengths we go to,
the subterfuge we cannot help
but see right through.

TUNNEL VISION

I am breaking the spine
of a new young poet –
a Faber first collection.

Circle Line stations
light up my progress –
circa two minutes between each

vertebra.
My eye is a camera obscura;
images entering through the lens

end up projected
on the retina
(or blind spot). But

how much experience
can be telescoped
into a stanza?

Light-years away
the unseen stars
care as little for poems

as chance remarks.
What do I burn for?
Degrees of fierceness

or indifference.
The odd flash
that catches an image

and reddens the eye;
flint-blue sparks
that spurt from a rail,

the fizz and crackle
of shooting stars
in the Angel dark.

NASTURTIUMS
Deniliquin, New South Wales, Australia

The hotter the summer, the more resolute she became,
stoking her beds of blood-orange flowers
as though blaze inflamed blaze face to face:
red-hot pokers, marigolds, pom-pom dahlias.
Along the fence a cordon of fibrous sunflowers
was spruce as the Salvation Army.
A moral triumph. All hers.

Watering was exhausting: she'd come in
flushed, smelling of crushed tomato leaves,
clutching a handful of nasturtiums.
I'd hear their torn-flame petals sizzle
as she doused stems in a pewter vase.

Once she teased me into tasting a leaf –
bitter, peppery. 'Astringent,' she said.
'Capers are an acquired taste, too.'
She even treated seedpods like spoils;
the larder's pickling jars were trussed
in gingham bonnets, stiff with wax.

Why did she go on sifting compost avidly
as a gold prospector panning silt?
Why did she make slits of her eyes,
a visor against blue glare,
and prick out tray after tray?

I resented the sun;
it made skin itch in the night
(worse than mosquitoes) and sting.
I wanted a cockatoo, sulphur-crested,
one I could teach to swear
at awkward moments, or guests;
one that would split sunflower seeds
and gouge a wedge of apple.
But a parrot was out of the question.
Psittacosis.

So while she staked gladioli,
I'd watch from the kitchen, leggy in shorts,
slicing the tops off Seville oranges –
an Indian, scalping. Then
I'd dip my lips in castor sugar,
kisses crusty as coldsores,
and suck flesh to a stringy pulp,
one by one, insatiable.

THE UNPAINTED ANGELS*

Our bodies are subtle, outlines
defined only by coarse pigments –
corrosion scraped from a copper plate,
crushed insects,
a mineral he used frugally
and called 'lapis lazuli'.
We're trapped like gnats stuck in gum
arabic – the underpainting's amber resin.

That symmetrical burial
isn't the way I remember it.
Too lyrical. Where are the flies,
where's that shifty baker with a hare-lip
and the whore oiling and coiling her hair,
hoping to cash in on rough trade?

In the preliminary drawings
he gave us leather sandals
(as if we could adjust a buckle pin
without it melting like an icicle)
and swathed us in drapes. Unendurable,
the weight and rasp of silk.
Their imagination is an encumbrance,
and they lay it on thick with palette knives.

The lunchtime lectures are killing.
Listen. How conscious the tour-guides are
of their delivery; and how pious –
taking themselves seriously
as those theologians who poured away their lives
in deserts of gritty calculation.
How much sinks in? Who now remembers
Dionysius the Areopagite
who knocked the choirs into shape –
Seraphim at the top, us at the bottom
in the celestial rankings?
We'd laugh – camels, needles and all that –
but they were serious. Deadly.

We know our place, and deference suits us.
But sometimes at night, after enduring
bad breath and the stench of dried egg
tempera all day, we're tempted to cut free,
to lift off and swoop through the galleries,
if only to tease a security camera
into winking one bloodshot eye.

---

* Two unfinished paintings by Michelangelo hang in Gallery 8 at the National
Gallery, London – *The Entombment* and *The Manchester Madonna*, in which two
unpainted angels stand behind the Virgin.

CHARGING FOR APPEARANCES

'You sow seed-pearls of doubt
in my mind, and turn our sheets
into an oyster bed, culturing poems.
Who knows where they'll be read?

And another thing – I never choose
when to enter, or exit, as Muse.
You pick on the most unlikely things;
not me
       rain be-spangled, deadheading a rose
       (I rather fancied that, like an album snap)

       or passionate as squid in the inky night
       (you never like my suggestions).

At the Norbiton Life Class,
(two electric bars in winter,
tea and bourbons in the breaks)
they stare at my various bits
like seagulls at washed up fish –
'objective' I think they called it.

All the would-be Lucian Freuds want

       electric light, splayed crotch,
       the abattoir aesthetic,

and budding Picassos always squash
both eyes on one side of my face, like plaice.

But what you do is surreptitious,
pickpocketing things I didn't know I had;
beachcombing when you should be out of your depth,
doing the breast stroke, fathoming me,
charting unknown waters with your compass needle.
Who knows what you'll scavenge next?'

THE ROOM OF PARROTS

No mustiness in the air.
No droppings grout the tiled floor.
Not even the ghosts of *pentimenti**
in the plasterwork.

They lived long, those long-tailed parrots,
chained to enamel perches,
offered pine kernels, cuttlebone,
bits of peach on the tip of a knife
in return for plumage
more opulent and more lavish
than gilded leather from Córdoba.

Now silence has coalesced.
In the Room of Parrots, light opens
and closes a canary fan each day,
and the frescos, restored, look on – bored
saints, schematic; a cardinal's faded hat,
skies of flaked ice.

But here, in this corner, on a gloved wrist,
a Hyacinth Macaw once pecked a ring,
gouged out the eye,
turned it in its beak and claw
as it would an emerald nut,
dropped it and screamed.

How do I know these things?

---

* *Pentimento* (plural *pentimenti*): Literally, repentance.
An alteration made by the artist to an area already painted.

In the Vatican *La Stanza del Pappagallo* was frescoed by Raphael, but damaged
soon after his death and badly restored. Every papal residence built since then
has had a Parrot Room.

DUTCH INTERIOR WITH YELLOW SILK

All morning she worked by the window,
prudent with the best of the light,
knotting a snowflake edging for a pillow,
her feet on a wooden box with a warm stone inside.

She peeled a dozen apples to help
the maid who'd scalded both her hands
tipping fish stock from a copper pan,
then turned the cheeses, thumbed their rinds.

No harpsichord lesson; today
silence was malleable as warm wax.
She opened windows as if each glazed pane
was a prayer – the closest she could get

to catching light mid-air – then sat
and counted out the chequered tiles,
black and white, white and black,
waiting like a mirror, without impatience,

for what she did not know would happen,
for the moment when a boy would bring
a bowl of pomegranates,
and by leaving them, change everything.

TIMESWITCH
Bologna Cathedral
For Stephen Oliver

Ranks of electric candles have been installed;
they save the vergers having to scrape
trays of congealed tears, crusty as pork dripping.

300 lira buys an unfaltering beam
from one of these miniature lighthouses;
their constancy is harsh
and dazzles like the circlet of stars
twined around the Virgin's halo
in earthed flex.

For you, who savoured austerity
and tiled the music room,
I choose hard wax;
brittle, translucent as fingernails –
not the soft tallow that melts like lard
and runs like warm Canadian honey.

I light its wick in another's flame –
and there you stand,
emblematic in a metal rack,
balanced at a dangerous angle,
lolling subversively in the parade,
burning the more fiercely for that.

You are still alight as I write this
in my hotel room, white sheets on white formica,
overlooking the market's fishstalls
where huge live prawns crawl,
their tailfins vivid as the angel's wings
in Fra Angelico's *Annunciation.*

I watch them, glistening mauve and yellow,
drying like new-hatched butterflies
brightened by an unfamiliar light.

'JUST LOOKING' IN THE HAIR-SHIRT SHOP *

What is she up to,
this po-faced nun,
suckling a hairy monkey?
Is it the pelican's blood-milk she dispenses
through a stiff nipple
with a selflessness that outdoes
the Abbess's two hundred full prostrations
in a wimple –
ordinary mortifications that embed
grit in chilblains and forehead?

Or hanky-panky?

We are the self-conscious ones,
trying on imagery to suit ourselves,
gazing in full-length mirrors
at various points of view,
appraising subtleties while she
goes on scowling through the centuries,
projecting one angular breast
through the Byzantine folds of her dress,

and the beast in her lap
goes on sucking, sucking.

* In *The Image on the Edge, the Margins of Medieval Art* by Michael Camille, there is
a marginal illustration from a Lancelot romance of a nun suckling a monkey.

FIVE GLASS EYES

I did not imagine it would be like this
quite – my neck braced in a horseshoe,
the angle of my head determined
not by the strength of my devotion
but something my husband calls *flair*.

He stands behind, among jardinières
and great swathes of palm.
Achieving a likeness, it seems,
requires a mastery of artifice.

I do not specially like this dress
but he does, and it is a serious piece
of needlework. Incontestably.
I chose only jet, and this brooch –
seed pearls surrounding a panel
woven with my grandmother's hair.

We have been posed and left here
while a glass plate is rinsed in silver.
We do not talk. It is like church,
being in the presence of a design
conceived to transcend time;
something that makes mortality
durable. Endurable.
     I am convinced
breeding will dignify the 'exposure' –
my carriage, my spine, the slope of my shoulders,
an oblique no less poised now
than when, refolding my Kashmiri shawl,
I used to catch the young men's eyes …
jackdaw eyes.
    Memory is fleet
compared with this discomfiture.
Interminable. Like posterity.

He said *Do not try to maintain a smile –*
a passing thing. It proves unsuitable.

SKIN-GRAFT FOR MARSYAS

He lay on sterilised sheets
in the emergency unit for burns;
two saline drips looped from a bedside stand.

The nurse arranged sedated limbs
as if for today's anatomy lecture.
Achilles tendons glistened,
thonging calf-muscle to bone;
ligaments were intricate
as tangled puppet-strings.
At his waist, pouches of fat –
small brooches of milky opal.

The surgeon checked the autoclave,
snapped into prophylactic gloves.
Delicate with forceps, he selected
segments of cultured skin
and matched the pigmentation.
His sutures in dissolving thread
were exemplary – painstaking.
Before his mother got glaucoma
she'd collected samplers –
pious sentiments, cross-stitched kisses;
even he'd admired the *petit point.*

But as Marsyas healed, he outgrew
the sheath constricting him –
a foreskin needing circumcision.
Scar tissue shrinks;
in his palms, skin ruched,
resisting scored designs –
the imposition of heart- and love-lines.
His fingertips were bald;
no nails, no moons, no whorls.

Stripped of their lids, eyes stare
like abattoir veal.
His new glass irises were cornflower;
each pupil's dilation had been calibrated
to endear.

Five times a day he sipped glucose
from a pipette, a raw pink fledgling;
intravenous drugs suppressed
the tissues' impulse to reject
and pain the surgeon called 'provisional'.

Given time, a physiotherapist
coaxed his fingers to uncurl –
scorpions learning to crawl –
and taught him to pick out his needs
on a keyboard.

It had been easy to improvise
on drilled stag's bone;
the marrow's empty cylinder had longed
to overflow with sound.
When he gave it breath it gave him melody
in return, as though he played a silver flute
or Pan's bound reeds.

There'd been no need to read,
to think *what is the fingering? ...*
now I must breathe, and now, and now ...
when finches flocked from the orchard
into the grove of olive trees
and fell silent
among the oleanders and laurel leaves.

Marsyas found the stag's bone flute which had been cursed and discarded by
Athene. Those who heard him play said even Apollo could not have made better
music with his lyre. Apollo challenged Marsyas to a contest which the Muses were
to judge. The contest proved an equal one until Apollo reversed his instrument
(which a flautist cannot do) and sang hymns to the Olympian gods. The Muses
gave the verdict in his favour. Apollo then tied Marsyas to a tree and flayed him.

A CORRESPONDENCE COURSE IN SINGING

I

If I am succinct
in this, my first letter,
it is because I expect as much
from you. The point is this:

you will become a surgeon
whose scalpel is your own voice,
and you will learn to operate
on the heart.

You must not tremble,
wielding this knife.
Learn the pattern of nerves,
and when I say 'Be incisive'
respect the skill that must go in
to making an incision.

Pulse is inseparable from ventricle;
the chambers of the human heart
are themselves a work of art.

II

On diction:
vowels must be mouthwatering,
marshmallow held over a flame,
and consonants crisp
as sticks of celery in iced water.

I am hungry, and listening.
Listening is hunger.
Do not set my teeth on edge
with a mouthful of sour rhubarb.

Attend to the inaudible –
the 'p' in *pterodactyl*,
the unvoiced *mmm* that must precede
explosive 'b's.

What's the first letter in *Beatus Vir?**

III

True legato depends on integrity,
not breath control.
When you no longer strive to impress,
when you are no longer riddled
with the ego's false humility,
a line will pour unbroken from your lips
like liquid from the lip of a vessel.
A blood vessel; a chalice.

Your ears, your lungs, will recognise
the flux of emptiness
only when it ceases; then
you'll tilt your head and close your eyes
as if in prayer, and long for more.

But truth, like legato, is not more
or less.
It is constancy. And selflessness.
And breath.

* Choral work by Monteverdi.

IV

Do not think of rhythm
as a pacemaker –
something you can insert
into a flagging interpretation.

Flamenco dancers quicken
clay into blood,
stamp out the stars
and strike new sparks,
ablaze with triumph, defiance,
the desolation of love.

What is it that impels their dance
towards its own extinction,
towards its own inertia?
Rhythm.

The Tarantella is the Dance of Death;
it springs again and again from the grave.

Do not think
of rhythm.

V

This new narcissism disgusts me.
You meet with cold approval
equal only to your merit.

If I teach at all,
I teach you to transcend
mimicry.
         Reflect on this
in silence.

I am your mirror.

Abuse me and I will shatter
your imagery.

VI

Sight-reading? Sight-singing?
Necessary skills,
but teaching them bores me.

Listen to birdsong –
priceless, and cheap –
for lessons in spontaneity.

A thrush will demonstrate
how best to improvise;
how startling

and inevitable
a cadenza should be.
How sparingly to ornament.

VII

Words aren't pearls, waiting
to be strung on your breath – a necklace
to complement your décolletage.

Poets and librettists can delete
their way towards poetry – let them
drill and polish every syllable;

you, in performance, must dissolve:
flow like ink. One of my students
stuttered whenever he tried to speak,

until I gave him *Dichterliebe** to sing.

VIII

If you're self-conscious,
get pissed. Or see a therapist.
This is not my concern.

At times you'll feel
more goose-pimples
than a tight-rope-walker in the nude.

Don't get your public,
and your private life,
confused:

seduce the ear,
risk grace, fall;
this has nothing whatever to do

with whether you choose
the life of a slattern
or a prude.

---

* *Poet's Love* : a song-cycle in which Schumann sets poems
from Heine's *Lyrisches Intermezzo*.

IX

You are young, and impatient.
I am old, but do I snatch at breath?

Time will slow to accommodate
an accomplished juggler.

Our element is time;
swim in it freely

as fish do in theirs.
You will find you do not drown.

X

An inland sea evaporates
and falls back into itself.
It is the same with song.

Do not imagine the vocal cords
condense breath into sound:
air is already sound

before you have breathed in
or out; just as vapour,
as it rises, is already rain.

XI

Persuade me,
without props or artifice,
that you *are*

> a jilted lover,
> a maiden spinning thread,
> a boy on horseback staring at Death.

Lose yourself in listening,
and blend like a chameleon.

The *ear* is the master of inflection,
not the intellect, or tongue.
Not even language. Or me.

Nuance is a subtle subterfuge,
but sickening as perfume
when overdone.

Originality?
One of the masks
worn by self-righteousness.
Like 'authenticity'.

XII

Are you a puppet, strung
on your own technique? – a dummy
dandled on a ventriloquist's knee?
Forbid yourself to imitate.

As a toddler you found your feet;
now find your voice. Speak –
not just to anyone –
to me.

There is no greater lie
than a recorded heartbeat
used to soothe a child to sleep.
Sing me Brahms's lullaby.

XIII

I have a great liking for figs.
Not dried – sweet ones,
with Parma ham.

Please send me two dozen;
they are especially good
this summer, I understand.

You ask about conductors.
Take no notice of anything
except the baton;

think of it as a silent bird
which must migrate
over glaciers, deserts, forests,

but whose wings are clipped
to the span of a human arm,
a human hand.

Give it voice;
this will require of you
a Saint's humility.

(Saints fail you know,
over and over and over again:
therein lies their sanctity.)

The blind use a white stick too,
and they *really* listen.
Tap tap tap. Remember that.

XIV

You assume too much.

For one thing, there are limits
to how much I can give;
you, in turn, must learn to forgive.

Besides, some questions
must remain questions
of taste.

After the breast comes the spoon,
after the spoon comes the hunger.
It is by hunger, now, that you will be fed.

XV

We disagree,
but that defines respect.
I am putting up my fees
and cutting back.

XVI

It is time you worked on songs
without words – Mendelssohn,
and Rachmaninov's *Vocalise*,
from memory:

but memory conceived
as past and future simultaneously –
inseparable as wind from air,
as waves from sea.

XVII

What do you mean,
I repeat myself?

I have changed, meantime,
and so have you.

A phrase, repeated,
never means the same –

at least in music,
or when I'm teaching.

XVIII

If what I say no longer seems
contradictory,
or cryptic,
you may forget

everything I've taught
except this:
diligence never did
transfigure bliss.

XIX

Some mornings when I feel
the ear yearns to be a little deaf,
a little more selective,
I think of selling my library –

everything but Schubert
and Schumann.
Bach.
And of course Mozart.

Do you like this postcard?*
See how he makes light modulate
across the surface of a glazed jug.
How can I teach that?

The gilded letters on the open lid
of the virginals read,
MUSIC IS A MEDICINE FOR GRIEF,
I think. It's hard to see.

---

* Johannes Vermeer (1632–75) *The Music Lesson* (also known as *A Lady
 with a Gentleman at the Virginals*), The Queen's Collection.

 Some of the painted text is concealed by the lady's head and shoulder,
 but a conjectural reading of the whole is:
 MVSICA LETITIÆ CO(ME)S MEDICINA DOLOR(IS).

XX

Audiences believe what they see.
What they see in me is serenity,
but I know it is the consequence
of a life-long preparation –

not for performance
or the consummation of applause,
not for floating a pianissimo
across a lake of heads,

but for the perfect cadence,
the last out-breath.
If I have given you anything
do not hoard it; pass it on ...

Performers are only trustees,
or curators in a vast museum,
guiding the public towards
whatever composers have achieved.

I have no heirlooms, only this
responsibility – to pass on
my lessons in how to inspire,
and how to expire.

GREGORY WARREN WILSON

Photograph: Hanya Chlala

Gregory Warren Wilson is the unanimous choice for the 1996 Staple FIRST EDITIONS award. Born in 1956, he trained for six years at the Royal Ballet School and later studied violin and composition at the Royal College of Music. He worked for one year with the Hong Kong Philharmonic and for two in Florence at the Opera House – positions which enabled him to deepen his interest in Oriental and Renaissance Art – before returning to London. He was a member of the Razumovsky String Quartet for three years, and the London Mozart Players for ten.

Warren Wilson won the *Tears in the Fence* Pamphlet Competition with the sequence of poems *Hanging Windchimes in a Vacuum,* due later this summer, which arose from a tour of Japan as a Western classical musician. This year he has also won the Lincolnshire Literature Festival Poetry Competition, and was awarded second prize for a *Remembered Place* poem by the Housman Society.

He has had one-man shows of his work as a visual artist in London, Sydney, Canberra and Melbourne. He collects nineteenth-century green-glass paperweights ('dumps'), made from leftover glass after a day's bottle-blowing, and lives in North London with an overgrown garden.

ACKNOWLEDGEMENTS

Some of the poems included in this collection first appeared in: Staple, *The Bound Spiral, Tees Valley Writer, Ver Verse* 1993, *West Sussex Gazette, Out of the Blue,* Blue Nose Poetry *Winners' Anthology* 1994, Helena Poetry Circle *Prize Winning and Shortlisted Poems* 1994, Ripley Poetry Association *Open Competition Anthology* 1995.

Cold Kiln won the Tees Valley Writer Competition; *The Water Table* won the Ripley Poetry Association Open Competition; *'Just Looking' in the Hair Shirt Shop* won the West Sussex Writers' National Competition. *English Miniaturist, Charging for Appearances,* and *Timeswitch* won second prizes in the Exeter, Barnet Borough, and Bournemouth International Festival competitions respectively. *The Missionary's Eel* and *Love Poem in the Form of a Bright Blue Soup Tureen* are from a group of ten poems which won the Blue Nose Poet of the Year award, 1994.

The engraving reproduced on the dedication page is *Limones minores* from Emanuel Sweerts, *Florilegium,* 1612.

Staple
and
Staple First Editions

Staple New Writing, established 1982, is published in March July and December of each year. Though Staple magazine has an entirely open policy, the monograph series Staple First Editions can only consider work which meets the published conditions.

Staple New Writing
Tor Cottage, 81 Cavendish Road, Matlock, Derbyshire DE4 3HD